THE RIEVAULX TERRACE

North Yorkshire

Here hills with vales, here woods with water vie;

Here art with nature strives to feast the eye;

Here Espec's tow'ring fabric, clad with green

And monkish grandeur, decorates the scene;

Here architects engrave th' Ionic scroll,

And fam'd Burnice's [Borgnis's] pencil crowns the whole.

ANON

National
Trust

Picture the Scene

'Ruins generally appear best from a distance.' That was the opinion of the writer Arthur Young, who came here in 1770. The Rievaulx Terrace was created about 1749–57 by Thomas Duncombe II to provide just such a distant view of the medieval abbey ruins in the valley below.

Duncombe would bring his guests over from nearby Duncombe Park to enjoy the landscape. As they walked along the curving Terrace, a carefully contrived series of thirteen different views of Ryedale and Rievaulx Abbey gradually unfolded. Duncombe also placed classical temples at either end of the Terrace with the care of a painter composing a landscape. For the Rievaulx Terrace was one of the earliest triumphs of the Picturesque movement in landscape gardening, which sought to re-create in nature the idealised pictures of artists like Claude and Poussin, yet still appear natural.

Like any garden visitor today, at the end of his tour Duncombe wanted something to eat. So the Ionic Temple was provided with a kitchen in the basement, from which he and his guests were served meals in the ornately decorated room above, sheltered from the Yorkshire breezes. In the 19th century the Ionic Temple also housed the gardener, who mowed the grass and sold tickets to visitors, who were welcome to see what Young called 'a bird's eye landscape, a casual glance at a little paradise'.

The Tuscan Temple from the far end of the Terrace

The Cistercian Abbey

On 5 March 1132 twelve monks arrived in the sheltered, fertile valley of the River Rye. Here they founded the first Cistercian abbey in the north of England under the protection of Walter Espec, the powerful Lord of Helmsley Castle two miles away. Their abbey prospered, particularly under the rule of the third abbot, St Aelred (1147–67), who began most of the buildings we see today. When the abbey was suppressed in 1538, Rievaulx and its lands were granted to Espec's descendant, Thomas Manners, Earl of Rutland, who began systematically demolishing the abbey buildings. However, because the Earl lived mainly at Belvoir Castle in Rutland, he did not attempt to convert the abbey into a house, and so much survived.

In 1632 the Rievaulx and Helmsley estates passed to the dissolute 2nd Duke of Buckingham, only to be confiscated by the Commonwealth, which gave them to Cromwell's Yorkshire general, Thomas Fairfax. However, Buckingham succeeded in retrieving them by marrying Fairfax's daughter, Maria. He died in 1687, childless and deep in debt, and seven years later the twin estates, which amounted to 40,000 acres, were sold, for the first and last time in their history, for the huge sum of £90,000.

Vistas cut through the woods frame a series of distinct views of Rievaulx Abbey and Ryedale

New Money: The Duncombes

The buyer was Sir Charles Duncombe (1648–1711), who had risen from obscurity to become Lord Mayor of London and the richest commoner in England. Apprenticed to a London goldsmith, he had moved into banking, and made a fortune financing the regimes of Charles II and James II as Cashier of Excise. Alexander Pope sneered:

Helmsley once proud Buckingham's delight
Slides to a scrivener [banker] or a City Knight.

Duncombe already had a mansion at Teddington and a Wiltshire estate at Downton, and would have stayed in Helmsley Castle when in the North. So little was done at Rievaulx. When he died in 1711, he left £400,000, but no will. The Helmsley estates passed to his sister Ursula Browne, who promptly settled them on her son, Thomas (?1683–1746).

Thomas was around 28 when he inherited and was determined to establish the family in North Riding society. In gratitude to his uncle, he not only changed his name to Duncombe, but also christened his vast new house Duncombe Park, in conscious rivalry with his grandest neighbours, the Howards of Castle Howard. The house was designed in 1713 by a Yorkshire squire, Sir William Wakefield, but its baroque silhouette may owe something to Vanbrugh, the architect of Castle Howard. The following year Thomas cemented his social position by marrying Sarah Slingsby, the sister of a Yorkshire baronet, Sir Henry Slingsby of Scriven. His own sister Mary made an even more prestigious match, marrying the 2nd Duke of Argyll, although the couple separated soon afterwards.

The Duncombe Terrace

Duncombe Park was built on a dramatic new site – the high plateau between Helmsley and Rievaulx. Thomas Duncombe exploited the terrain by excavating a curved, grassy terrace south of the house, which offers spectacular views down to the estate's traditional heart, Helmsley Castle. A statue of Father Time in the centre of the terrace underlined the contrast between old and new. At either end of the terrace are classical temples. The open Ionic rotunda was probably built in 1718 by Vanbrugh. He was in Yorkshire that year, and it is almost identical to the rotunda he put up at Stowe in Buckinghamshire three years later. The circular Doric temple probably came slightly later, and may have been inspired by Hawksmoor's Mausoleum at Castle Howard.

The terrace itself was created between about 1713 and 1718 and so predates by a decade the similar terrace walk at Castle Howard. There is no surviving evidence of who designed the Duncombe Terrace, but it may have been the royal gardener Charles Bridgeman, who was working in the North Riding at the time. The formality of the straight-edged yew hedges and avenues is typical of his style at this date, and the serpentine ha-ha recalls his contemporary work at Stowe. This novel feature allowed unrestricted views over the surrounding landscape, while the fortress-like bastions were perhaps meant to echo the medieval castle below. The Duncombe Terrace comes at the end of a tradition of formal gardening which the more relaxed style of the Rievaulx Terrace superseded.

Duncombe Park was designed for Thomas Duncombe I in 1713; engraving from Vitruvius Britannicus (1725)

The Duncombe Terrace

(*Opposite*)
Thomas Duncombe I sits surrounded by his family. Standing on the left is his eldest son, Thomas II, who built the Rievaulx Terrace. Painted by Andrea Soldi, 1741 (Duncombe Park)

Thomas Duncombe II and the creation of the Rievaulx Terrace

Thomas Duncombe's son, also called Thomas, inherited in 1746 at the age of about 22. The following year he made the Grand Tour, like many wealthy young men of the time, visiting Florence and Venice. The journey left him with a love of Antique statuary and Old Master paintings, and also earned him election to the Society of Dilettanti, a club for aristocratic art-lovers who had been to Italy. He enhanced his social position still further in 1749, when he married Lady Diana Howard, the daughter of the 4th Earl of Carlisle, the owner of Castle Howard. Thanks to his father-in-law, he became MP for Morpeth, and the marriage seems to have inspired him hugely to extend the Duncombe Park landscape. For around 1749 he began constructing a second great terrace as a companion to his father's, overlooking the abbey ruins at Rievaulx. According to an old 'List of Remarkable Occurrences' transcribed by the local 19th-century antiquarian Thomas Parker: '1757, The Terrace at Rievaulx Bank Top was finished, being worked at about eight years.'

Duncombe may have originally intended to link the Rievaulx Terrace more directly with Duncombe Park. Large piles of dressed masonry have been found in the combe through which the road climbs from Rievaulx to Helmsley. This suggests that he planned to build a huge viaduct right across this valley, enabling his guests to drive the three miles from one terrace to the other with panoramic views from the escarpment all the way. But in the event, he decided against it.

Who designed the Temples?

It is not certain who designed the Rievaulx Terrace or the temples at either end of it. The most likely candidate is Sir Thomas Robinson, a Yorkshire gentleman-architect who was married to the 3rd Earl of Carlisle's daughter, and who rebuilt the west wing of Castle Howard for his father-in-law. Thanks to his friendship with Lord Burlington, who designed the York Assembly Rooms, Robinson was in the forefront of the Palladian movement, and immensely self-confident on architectural matters: having commissioned Sir William Wakefield to rebuild his own family home, Rokeby Park, he decided to do the job himself. He was particularly interested in round temples like those on the Duncombe and Rievaulx terraces.

Later History

Thomas Duncombe II died in 1799, and the property passed first to his brother and then to his nephew, who was created Lord Feversham in 1826. His grandson William was in turn advanced to an Earldom in 1868, having commissioned Sir Charles Barry to make large additions to Duncombe Park in 1843–6. Unfortunately, the main block was badly damaged by fire in 1879, and the north wing was destroyed by another fire in 1894. The present house is a complete rebuilding, based, externally, on the original Wakefield design. The National Trust acquired the Rievaulx Terrace and its two temples in 1972. Duncombe Park is once again the family home of the Fevershams, who open it to the public.

Sir Thomas Robinson, the probable architect of the Rievaulx temples; painted by Frans van der Mijn, 1750 (National Portrait Gallery)

The Ionic Temple

The Tuscan Temple

The Taste for Gothic Ruins

The abbey ruins at their most romantic; engraving by George Cuitt, 1825

Ah then most happy, if thy vale below
Wash, with the crystal coolness of its rills,
Some mould'ring abbey's ivy-vested wall.

William Mason, *The English Garden* (1772)

For two centuries after the Dissolution of the Monasteries, many of the ruins were left to decay. But in the 1720s the antiquaries Samuel and Nathaniel Buck began to record what was left in a series of engravings which created a new interest in abbey ruins. In his influential garden at The Leasowes near Halesowen in Shropshire in 1745–63 William Shenstone built a Gothic ruined abbey which could be viewed from key points in the tour of his landscape. Nearby, at Hagley in Worcestershire, Sanderson Miller also designed a brand new ruin in the Gothic style, which Horace Walpole admired as showing 'the true rust of the Barons' wars'.

The Rievaulx Terrace was partly inspired by the Studley Royal landscape garden, which offered similarly picturesque views down to the ruins of Fountains Abbey; coloured engraving by Anthony Walker, 1758

Walpole shared his friend William Mason's passion for monastic ruins, and with his novel, *The Castle of Otranto* (1765), and his villa at Strawberry Hill he made all things Gothic fashionable again.

The most direct inspiration for the Rievaulx Terrace was probably provided by another famous Cistercian ruin in Yorkshire, Fountains Abbey. In 1730 John Aislabie extended his water garden at Studley Royal to take in a view of Fountains (although his son William did not acquire the actual abbey stones until 1768). And just as at Rievaulx, the natural topography provided a bird's-eye view of the abbey nestling in the valley of the River Skell. There were also family connections. Thomas Duncombe I's brother-in-law Sir Henry Slingsby was married to Aislabie's daughter, Mary, and it was thanks to Aislabie that Thomas I became MP for Ripon in 1734.

This 18th-century watercolour shows the Ionic Temple isolated on the Terrace, before Thomas Duncombe II's woodland planting had matured

The Rievaulx temples and valley landscape were meant to recall to the knowledgeable viewer the idealised visions of artists like Claude (*left*) and Salvator Rosa

Tour of the Terrace

The Temple of Vesta at Tivoli, which inspired innumerable colonnaded rotundas; engraving from the 1721 Leoni edition of Palladio's *Four Books*

From the car-park, you follow a woodland walk that emerges on to the wide grass lawn at the southern end of the Terrace, which is dominated by a circular temple.

The Tuscan Temple

Columned rotundas of this kind can be traced back to a single classical building – the Temple of Vesta at Tivoli near Rome. It inspired buildings as famous as St Paul's Cathedral in London and the Jefferson Memorial in Washington. The Temple of Vesta was illustrated in all the early 18th-century English translations of Andrea Palladio's *Four Books of Architecture* (1570) and so was well-known to English Palladian architects like Sir Thomas Robinson, who probably designed the Tuscan Temple in the late 1750s.

Thomas Duncombe II's Rievaulx rotunda is very similar to that built by his father at Duncombe. The main differences are that it stands on a podium rather than on a set of steps, and that the columns have no bases. For these reasons, it has always been known as the Tuscan Temple, but this is in fact incorrect: the entablature above, with its triglyphs, rams' skulls and plain rosettes, is unmistakably Doric, and the columns belong to the baseless Roman Doric order. This order was rarely used in England before the mid-18th century, when it became popular with sophisticated architectural taste. As such, it was one of the earliest expressions of Neo-classicism, which sought to interpret classical forms more faithfully. John Aislabie had chosen just such baseless Doric columns for his

The very similar Doric temple at Duncombe stands on a set of steps, rather than a podium

The Tuscan Temple from the far end of the Terrace

Temple of Piety at Studley Royal, built around 1730.

Much of the soft York stone from which the Tuscan Temple was made has had to be replaced.

The Interior
The rich plasterwork decorating the inside of the dome, together with the masks and drapes over the windows, were perhaps by the Italian plasterer Giuseppe Cortese, who was doing similar work in the Temple of Piety at Studley Royal in the late 1740s. In the centre of the dome is a painted roundel of a winged goddess, which is attributed to another Italian craftsman, Andrea Casali (1700–84). Casali was encouraged to come to England in 1741 by Thomas Duncombe II's father-in-law, the 4th Earl of Carlisle, who employed him at Castle Howard. He also worked not far away at Hovingham.

On the floor is part of a 13th-century tesselated pavement supposedly found near the high altar of the Abbey in 1821, and relaid here as nearly as possible in its original arrangement. Look out for the carving of the door- and window-cases, which is particularly crisp. The octagonal table in the centre of the room has an early 17th-century Italian marble top on a modern base.

The interior decorator John Fowler suggested the present colour scheme, which picks out the plasterwork in white against two shades of pale blue, about 1960. The colours were taken, at the last Earl of Feversham's request, from a pair of Sèvres vases at Sledmere.

Two other variations on the circular temple

Nicholas Hawksmoor's Mausoleum at Castle Howard

The Temple of Ancient Virtue at Stowe, which was built by William Kent in 1737

The Terrace

The idea of a hillside walk, giving magnificent views over a historic landscape and ending with garden buildings, was developed from 1739 by Sanderson Miller at Radway in Warwickshire, where he constructed a terrace and Gothic tower overlooking the Civil War battlefield of Edgehill, with the positions of the two armies indicated by clumps of trees. But Rievaulx represents a new departure in that it rejects the traditional idea of formal vistas. Instead of being led in a straight line from one garden feature to the next, you follow a gentle serpentine course, half a mile in length, during which different picturesque views gradually unfold. Every attempt is made to hide the fact that this landscape is man-made: the Terrace is backed by an undulating plantation of hardwoods mixed with flowering shrubs, while more woods beneath drop steeply down to the abbey and villages, unlike the even grass banks of Duncombe. The temples at each end are placed not so much as eye-catchers, but as incidentals in the landscape, like the buildings in a painting by Claude.

As you walk back along the Terrace from the Tuscan Temple, you should stop at the thirteen 'stations' to take in the thirteen distinct views cut through the trees below the Terrace. The first of these views, from the colonnade of the Tuscan Temple itself, looks down through the woods to the 18th-century bridge crossing the River Rye, a reconstruction of the original medieval packhorse bridge swept away by a flood in 1754. The second vista reveals the abbey cloisters and outbuildings; by the next, the three tall lancet windows of the chancel appear in direct line with the central tower. Further along the Terrace, new views open up across the valley to stone farmhouses and cottages on the far ridge and to the pools along the river. Halfway along the Terrace is a pair of gate piers, which were the original entrance to the Rievaulx Terrace from Duncombe.

With each clearing in the trees, the church is seen from a slightly different angle, like a piece of giant sculpture. The final view is at the far end of the terrace, from the steps of the Ionic Temple. This is the steepest drop of all – down to the great nave of the abbey.

Rievaulx Abbey from the Tuscan Temple end of the Terrace

(*Opposite*) The chancel of Rievaulx Abbey from the Ionic Temple end of the Terrace

The Ionic Temple

The Temple of Fortuna Virilis in Rome, one of the inspirations for the Ionic Temple; engraving from the 1721 Leoni edition of Palladio's *Four Books*

The interior of the Ionic Temple

The Ionic Temple

At the far northern end of the Terrace is a rectangular temple with an Ionic portico, again probably designed by Robinson in the late 1750s. Like the Tuscan Temple, this has a classical Roman source – the Maison Carrée at Nîmes, which was much admired by Hawksmoor, Robinson's rival at Castle Howard, as well as by later Neo-classicists. It is also indebted to the Temple of Fortuna Virilis in the Roman Forum, which was equally well known from English editions of Palladio. The restored plaster-work ceiling of the portico looks back to the work of Inigo Jones, the early 17th-century father of English Palladianism.

The Interior

The magnificent interior, with its table setting of Chamberlain Worcester porcelain, comes as something of a surprise after the comparative austerity of the classical exterior. Thomas Duncombe II wanted the building to have a practical function, as a banqueting house or a place to rest after the drive from Duncombe Park. In 1783 it was equipped to serve roast meat and sauces, wine and beer, followed by fruit, tea and coffee (with cream and sugar).

The chief glory of the room is the ceiling, which is frescoed with mythological scenes taken from Italian Baroque master-pieces. They are the work of the Italian painter Giuseppe Mattia Borgnis (1701–61), who came to England about 1753 and was soon busy decorating Sir Francis Dashwood's house, West Wycombe Park in Buckinghamshire. Dashwood was also a member of the Society of Dilettanti and probably recommended Borgnis to Duncombe. The frescos at Rievaulx are very similar to his work at West Wycombe.

In the centre of the ceiling is *Aurora, Apollo and the Muses*, based on Guido Reni's mural in the Palazzo Rospigliosi in Rome. In the rectagular compartments of the cove are four pairs of classical lovers: (from left to right) *Peleus and Thetis, Diana and Endymion, Perseus and Andromeda* and *Hercules and Omphale*. They were based on Annibale Carracci's famous ceiling in the Palazzo Farnese in Rome (1597–1600). In the circular medallions are four more pairs of mythological figures: *Boreas and Orithyia, Pan and Cupid, Hero and Leander,* and *Jupiter and Europa*. Fuller details are given on the sheet in the room.

The marble chimneypiece is in the style of a leading English sculptor of the mid-18th century, Henry Cheere. The present decoration was carried out by the last Earl of Feversham in the late 1940s. It re-creates that seen by Arthur Young in 1770, when the room was 'ornamented with gilt carving on a brown ground'.

Furniture

The set of twelve mid-18th-century mahogany dining-chairs was probably made for this room by a leading York cabinet-maker in the 1750s. The rest of the furniture was provided by the last Earl of Feversham. The most important piece is the pair of superb gilt settees, which came from the set designed about 1740 by William Kent for the famous Double Cube Room at Wilton House in Wiltshire.

The Basement

The two rooms here were originally used by servants to prepare food for the guests above.

Top The central ceiling fresco depicting Aurora, Apollo and the Muses

Middle left Peleus and Thetis

Middle right Diana and Endymion

Bottom left Perseus and Andromeda

Bottom right Hercules and Omphale

Flora and Fauna

In 1802 Dorothy Wordsworth, the sister of the poet, paid a visit to Rievaulx: 'Thrushes were singing, cattle feeding among green-grown hillocks about the ruins. These hillocks were scattered over with grovelets of wild roses and other shrubs, and covered with wild flowers.' Rievaulx remains a haven for wildlife and plants. Sparrowhawks swoop along the vistas, hunting for small birds, which feed among the rowans, hawthorns and blackberries. Pipistrelle, noctule and brown long-eared bats are a common sight at dusk. Purple wild orchids flower briefly in spring on the Terrace bank, and bluebells, wood anemones, forget-me-nots and wild garlic thrive under the tree canopy.

Looking after the Landscape
The National Trust aims to maintain the balance between the natural and man-made landscape which underlies Thomas Duncombe II's Picturesque creation. A continuing programme of tree-felling and replanting around the Terrace allows a more diverse age range of trees to develop. Young ash, oaks and lime trees have been planted to replace some of the losses due to Dutch Elm and Beech bark disease. Some dead timber is left in the woodland to provide food and shelter for many species of wildlife. The grassy bank is managed as traditional meadow, allowing wild flowers and butterflies to flourish. Great care is taken to protect small mammals when the grass is cut in late summer.

A sparrowhawk

Further Reading

ANON., 'Duncombe Park', *Country Life*, 25 February 1905, pp.270–8.

BECKETT, Sir Martyn, 'The Duncombe and Rievaulx Terraces', *Ryedale Historian*, vii, 1974, pp.3–8.

CAMPBELL, Colen, *Vitruvius Britannicus*, London, 1725, iii, pl.85–8.

CROFT-MURRAY, Edward, *Decorative Painting in England 1537–1837*, London, 1970, ii.

GILL, Thomas, *Vallis Eboracensis, comprising the History and Antiquities of Easingwold and its Neighbourhood*, London, 1852.

HUSSEY, Christopher, 'Duncombe Park, Yorkshire', *Country Life*, 5, 12 December 1957, pp.1198–1201, 1328–31.

HUSSEY, Christopher, *English Gardens and Landscapes 1700–1750*, London, 1967, pp.140–6.

PARKER, Thomas, 'History of Kirkdale with the towns and villages adjacent', *Ryedale Historian*, xi, 1982, p.19.

PATON, David, *Giuseppe Mattia Borgnis: The Cultural World of an Eighteenth-century Painter* (Cambridge MA thesis, 1984).

YOUNG, Arthur, *A Six Months Tour through the North of England*, London, 1770, ii, pp.87–94.

WORSLEY, Giles, 'The baseless Roman Doric column in mid-eighteenth century English architecture: a study in neo-classicism', *Burlington Magazine*, cxxviii, May 1986, pp.331–9.

WORSLEY, Giles, 'Duncombe Park, Yorkshire', *Country Life*, 24, 31 May 1990, pp.116–21, 138–43.

Photographs: British Architectural Library, RIBA, London pp.10 (top left), 14 (top left); Country Life Picture Library pp.5 (bottom), 10 (bottom left); Lord Feversham: Duncombe Park Collection p.4; National Portrait Gallery p.7 (top); National Trust p.5 (top); National Trust Images: p.8 (bottom), John Bethell p.1, Andrew Butler p.11 (bottom), Joe Cornish pp.3 (bottom right), 6, 7 (bottom), 10 (bottom right), 12, John Hammond p.9 (bottom), Andrea Jones front cover, pp.2–3, 13 (top and bottom), David Kjaer/BBC Natural History Unit Picture Library p.16, Nadia Mackenzie pp.14 (bottom left), 15 (all); Phillips p.9 (top right); Jenny Richenberg p.8 (top left); © Royal Commission on the Historical Monuments of England p.11 (top right); Wakefield Museums, Galleries and Castles back cover.

Printed by Acorn Press for National Trust (Enterprises) Ltd, Heelis, Kemble Drive, Swindon, Wilts SN2 2NA on Cocoon Silk made from 100% recycled paper

The National Trust

is a registered charity

is independent of government

was founded in 1895 to preserve places of historic interest or natural beauty permanently for the benefit of the nation

relies on the generosity of its supporters, through membership subscriptions, gifts, legacies and the contribution of many thousands of volunteers

protects and opens to the public over 300 parks, houses, gardens and ancient monuments and nature reserves

owns almost 250,000 hectares (618,000 acres) of the most beautiful countryside and nearly 750 miles of outstanding coast for people to enjoy

If you would like to become a member or make a donation, please telephone 0344 800 1895 (minicom 0344 800 4410); write to National Trust, PO Box 574, Rotherham S63 3FH; or visit our website at www.nationaltrust.org.uk

This guide draws on that written by the late Gervase Jackson-Stops in 1978. National Trust is particularly grateful to Lord Feversham, Jenny Richenberg, Mark Sayers and York City Art Gallery for their help.

(*Back cover*) The abbey ruins from the Ionic Temple; engraved by William Westall in 1819, when the Rievaulx Terrace was already a popular tourist attraction

ISBN 978-1-84359-289-1

9 781843 592891 >